Anonymous

Sites for Homes and Industries on the Western Maryland

Railroad

Anonymous

Sites for Homes and Industries on the Western Maryland Railroad

ISBN/EAN: 9783337419332

Printed in Europe, USA, Canada, Australia, Japan

Cover: Foto ©ninafisch / pixelio.de

More available books at **www.hansebooks.com**

SITES FOR HOMES

WESTERN

If, as I take it, a home is a place to live in, it should, above all things, be healthfully located. Look out, then, for two things—elevation and pure water.

Elevations *en route* Western Maryland R. R.: Arlington, 432 feet ; Reisterstown (Glyndon), 660 feet ; Westminster, 726 feet ; Linwood, 410 feet ; Monterey, 1400 feet ; Hanover, 607 feet.

The trustees of leading public institutions have evidently investigated the sanitary features of this region, for here on the Western Maryland are located Mt. Hope Retreat, Thomas Wilson Sanitarium and McDonogh Farm School.

Fruit belt on west slope of Blue Ridge wonderfully productive. Bearing term of peach trees thirty years or more. Farms pay for themselves in one year. Only three hours from Baltimore markets.

Frederick and Carroll counties—a fine grazing country ; fine sites for dairy farms. Good wheat lands for half the price of Pennsylvania lands.

Lumber much cheaper here, near the mountains.

Land in Hagerstown near the railroad offered *free*, for manufacturing purposes.

Town lots at Williamsport, excellently located, from $25 to $600.

Among the advantages for manufacturers along the Western Maryland R. R., I note : 1—Abundant water power. 2—Good mail facilities. 3—Proximity to the Baltimore markets. 4—Same through rates to points south and west that apply to Baltimore. 5—These much less than Philadelphia or New York rates. 6—Cheap living, cheap fuel, cheap labor.

ΙNTRODUCTION.

In editing and publishing the following letters, correspondence and memoranda of Mr. A. P. PENROSE, the Western Maryland R. R. has aimed to put in clear and readable shape such facts as would especially interest real estate investors, or those looking for sites for manufactories or country homes. The careful observations of a thoroughly practical man carry with them more weight than any set description can, and these observations are supplemented by building plans, lists of property owners, property and approximated prices of same, together with special rates and inducements offered by the Company to settlers along the Western Maryland line of road.

As the various "wild cat" speculations of the day show themselves in their true colors, wise and conservative investors turn more and more to real estate as the surest equivalent for hard cash. Banks break, "trusts" are not to be trusted, stocks "vanish in thin air and leave not a rack behind," but real estate in a healthful, beautiful locality, on a progressive and prosperous line of road, is as sure as anything in this world of ours can be. This book puts the facts and figures simply and clearly, and brings those who wish to buy and those who wish to sell into easy communication.

In a book entitled "Jaunts," which may properly be called the companion work of this, may be found a sketch of each station along the entire line of the Western Maryland R. R. and its branches, in regular order; and so concise, convenient and systematic is the arrangement, that the reader can, in less than three minutes, put himself in possession of all the principal matters of information concerning any part of the line. This book may be had at the office of the General Passenger Agent, and will be found an invaluable assistant to the person who is in earnest in his purpose to do the best possible thing for himself in securing a pleasant rural home, or an advantageous locality for farm or factory.

DESIGN No. 430.

BY THE CO-OPERATIVE BUILDING PLAN ASSOCIATION, ARCHITECTS.

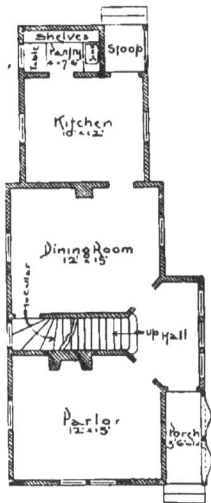

First Floor Plan.

Second Floor Plan.

SIZE OF STRUCTURE—Front, 20 ft.; Side, 44 ft.

ACCOMMODATIONS—Six rooms, also porch, hall, pantry, closets and cellar.

HEIGHT OF STORIES—Cellar, 6 ft., 6 in.; First Story, 8 ft., 6 in.; Second Story, 8 ft.

MATERIALS—Foundation, stone and brick; First Story, shingles; Second Story, shingles; Gables, shingles; Roof, shingles.

SPECIAL FEATURES—Can be built on a 25-foot lot, leaving space for a passage to the rear. The shingled porch, with its flower shelves, makes an attractive entrance. Open fire-place in the parlor. Flue for a stove in the dining-room.

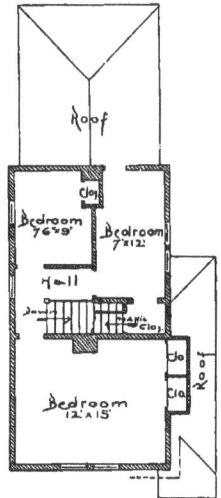

THE COST about $1,500. Further information concerning this design may be obtained free, by applying to the Co-operative Building Plan Association, Architects, 63 Broadway, N. Y.

4

LETTERS

BLUE MOUNTAIN, Md., July 15th, 1888.

————————, Esq.

DEAR SIR:—I have made the complete tour of the Western Maryland R. R., main line and branches, since you saw me off from Hillen Station four days ago, and am now returned to this charming spot—my original destination —to enjoy to the full my season of summer vacation. "The complete tour!" I hear you repeat in wonder. Yes; you see, by the time I had reached my purposed stopping place among the mountains, the trip had awakened to practical intent an idea that has for some time been lazily dreaming in my brain, of selecting

A SITE FOR A COUNTRY HOME.

This has induced me to explore the main line to its extreme point at Williamsport, Md., and the branches beside that run up into Pennsylvania. It was soon accomplished, but never, I think, was so much to charm the eye and please the fancy crowded into so short a time and space. For the continuous panorama of exquisite scenery it presents to view in a marvelously brief time, the Western Maryland is certainly the peer of any road over which I have traveled—and you know I am no stay-at-home. Bear in mind that the point I was bound for, the Blue Ridge Summit, is less than three hours' distance from Baltimore, the shortest by any road. Not only is this the nearest route to the mountains for Baltimore but for Philadelphia as well, which, by way of Baltimore, is only 167 miles, whereas, in his own State, to reach the nearest point in the Alleghanies, Cresson Springs, the Philadelphian must make a run of 200 miles and more. And let me assure you that an extra hour on train-board, in a hot and dusty season, especially if through a flat country, counts

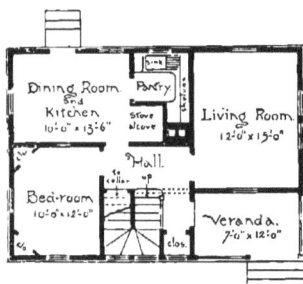

First Floor Plan.

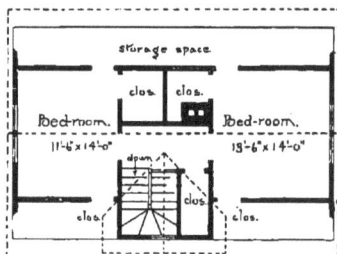

Second Floor Plan.

DESIGN No. 514.

BY THE CO-OPERATIVE BUILDING PLAN ASSOCIATION, ARCHITECTS.

SIZE OF STRUCTURE—Front, 34 ft.; Side, 23 ft., 6 in.

ACCOMMODATIONS—Six rooms, porch, veranda, closets, cellar.

HEIGHT OF STORIES—Cellar, 6 ft.; First Story, 9 ft.; Second Story, 8 ft.

MATERIALS—Foundation, stone wall; First Story, pine siding; Roof and Gables, shingles.

THE COST about $1,500. Further information concerning this design may be obtained free, by applying to the Co-operative Building Plan Association, Architects, 63 Broadway, N. Y.

for something in discomfort. I enjoyed, however, in the case of my present journey, a perfect immunity from such possible annoyance, and almost from the beginning was able to inflate my lungs with the

PURE UPPER AIR,

for the face of the country begins to rise with the setting out of the train, one may say, and continues steadily up, up, up, till we reach the mountain top. As a consequence of the fine elevation, I take it that there is not a point on this line whose general healthfulness is not assured, and that people who claim to know, tell the plain truth when they say that

NO MALARIAL DISORDERS

have a rag of a chance to distil their poison anywhere within earshot of its train whistle.

Thus, at Arlington, only seven miles from the city, we attain an altitude of 432 feet, after passing through a lovely country, abounding in thriving farms and pretty homes. People may here enjoy a healthful and beautiful home, as accessible to the centre of Baltimore as if it were upon the city boundaries. Many have already availed themselves of this double advantage, quite a number of handsome new cottages having been erected here, and also at Oakland, a little way farther back. A ride on train-board of little more than fifteen minutes, lands the city business man at a rural home in either of these villages —less time than it would take him to ride in the horse cars from his store or office to a town residence of two or more miles' distance.

Just here, *a propos*, for your fuller enlightenment on a matter which you, I know, like myself, have had under advisement, I insert, between my own pages, a letter received to-day from a friend with whom I have recently discussed the subject, who has also been exploring, and quite minutely, in the locality he mentions.

ARLINGTON, Md., July 14th, 1888.

——————, Esq.

My Dear Sir:—Doubtless you are surprised to learn that I am still "lingering, loth to leave" this beautiful country, and conclude that I have become infatuated with the hills and dales, mountains and meadows of "Maryland, my Maryland." But I write now not of charming scenery but of strictly business matters. I stepped off an early train from Baltimore this morning, and, *incog* and untrammeled, have devoted a day very pleasantly and, I think, very profitably, to a careful survey of the ground.

7

DESIGN No 434.

BY THE CO-OPERATIVE BUILDING PLAN ASSOCIATION, ARCHITECTS.

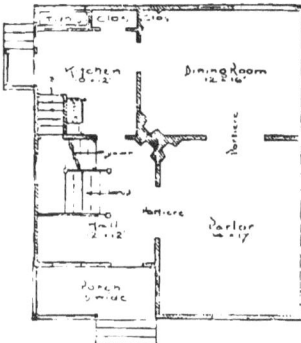

First Floor Plan.

SIZE OF STRUCTURE—Front, 27 ft., 6 in.; Side, 30 ft., 6 in.

ACCOMMODATIONS—Seven rooms, hall, cellar, closets, etc.

HEIGHT OF STORIES—Cellar, 6 ft., 6 in.; First Story, 9 ft.; Second Story, 8 ft.

MATERIALS—Foundation, stone; First Story, clap-boards; Second Story, shingles; Gables, shingles; Roof, shingles.

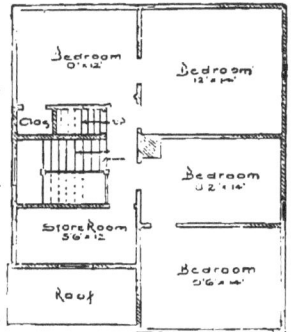

Second Floor Plan.

THE COST about $2,000. Further information concerning this design may be obtained free, by applying to the Co-operative Building Plan Association, Architects, 63 Broadway, N. Y.

The first thing that impresses me is that it takes only seventeen minutes to run from Union Station to this point—less time than is required to go from the centre of the city to many of the popular and fashionable residence sections of the town by the tedious horse-car lines. Just think of it; before you could reach some portions of Eutaw Place, or Franklin Square, or Lafayette Square from the business parts of the city, you could board a train at Union Station and climb right up, through green fields and over babbling brooks, past pleasing landscapes and pretty cottages, to Arlington, 432 feet above tide water. Can you realize it? Let me make a comparison. The high-service reservoir in Druid Hill Park, only one mile from Arlington, that supplies water to the most elevated portions of the city, is so far below this, that could you jump from this elevation directly into the water you would have performed an exploit greater than that of the man who jumped from the Brooklyn bridge. Again: if you could look down on Washington's monument from this elevation, you would be as far above the statue of Washington on its summit as the bronze lion (that has been waiting so patiently for him to "come down" and be eaten) is beneath him.

Arlington is situated on a ridge, or rather an elevated plateau, about equidistant from Gwynn's Falls on the south and the historic Jones on the north, while through the centre runs the Western Maryland, being at this point about two miles from either water-course. Geologists have found this area an interesting field for study. A member of the Johns Hopkins has lately contributed a valuable paper on the "trap," or, more familiarly, "niggerhead" rocks of this section. They are said to be of igneous origin, hence much older than the surrounding gneiss that occupies all this portion of the State. But don't get impatient; I do not mean to give you a lecture on rocks, except to refer to their value for building and paving.

The new city line crosses the railroad about 100 yards below Arlington station and forms the southwest corner near this point. The country around is being rapidly built up, as the people think, but this is nothing to the boom I predict for this place and several miles beyond as soon as its advantages for residences are better known. A gentleman here, who has several cottages rented out, told me that he seldom had to advertise them, as they were applied for as soon as they were vacant; and it was his opinion that a thousand cottages distributed along the road as far as Pikesville could be rented as soon as finished.

DESIGN No. 203.

BY THE CO-OPERATIVE BUILDING PLAN ASSOCIATION, ARCHITECTS.

First Floor Plan.

Second Floor Plan.

SIZE OF STRUCTURE—Front, 24 ft., 6 in.; Side, 35 ft., inclusive of veranda.

ACCOMMODATIONS — Seven rooms, also veranda, hall, closets, pantry and bath.

HEIGHT OF STORIES—Cellar, 6 ft., 6 in.; First Story, 9 ft.; Second Story, 8 ft., 3 in.; Third Story, open attic.

MATERIALS—Foundation, stone; First Story, clap-boards; Second Story, shingles; Gables, paneled; Roof, shingled.

SPECIAL FEATURES—A cellar under the whole house, with access to it from the kitchen. A stairway to the attic is provided, where two good rooms can be finished if desired. Wide openings between the hall, parlor and dining room make these apartments very attractive and roomy. The central and corner windows of the dining room give a beautiful bay-window effect to that apartment.

THE COST about $2,500. Further information concerning this design may be obtained free, by applying to the Co-operative Building Plan Association, Architects, 63 Broadway, N. Y.

Land can be had here in lots of an acre or less for $500 to $2000 per acre; and in tracts of 50 to 100 or more acres for $250 to $1000 per acre. There is a big speculation here for somebody in buying a large tract of land at a low figure, laying off a village, and selling it out in lots at a large profit. I have visited the principal cities in the Union, but nowhere have I seen land so advantageously situated—so near and so accessible to a large city, so salubrious, and purchasable at so low a rate.

The Arlington Savings and Loan Association, an excellent institution doing business here, enables men of limited means to become owners of comfortable and pretty homes that otherwise they could never have possessed. Let me give an illustration: A man who pays twenty-five dollars per month for a city house comes out to Arlington and selects a desirable half acre or more, valued at $600, on which he erects one of the beautiful cottages designed by Shoppel, costing $2000. For this he lays out $9.10 cash, and borrows the balance of $10.90 from the building association, for which he pays in principal and interest just about twenty dollars per month, five dollars less than his rent in the city. This amount constantly decreases until, at the expiration of ten years (at which time his house will be paid for), he will be paying only about thirteen dollars per month. Meanwhile, besides the comfort of living under "his own vine and fig tree," with the additional health and happiness secured by a trifling outlay and an amount of labor that is but a pleasant diversion, his home could be transformed into a paradise of roses, grape vines and fruit trees, with all those little settings that make a home worth having. In addition to all this, the Western Maryland R. R., after helping to move all his building material, gives him a free ride over the road to and from the city one year for every $1000 expended in improvements.

Many of the substantial business men of Baltimore have recognized the claims of this section as a place of residence, and their neat and elegant homes may be seen on every hand. I tell you, my dear sir, there is a great future for the section of country lying along the Western Maryland R. R. from Baltimore many miles out, and I prophesy that the boom will start at or near the city limits, and the county I have visited to-day will be the first to feel it.

Can't we seize this opportunity, and by feebly assisting the movement, abundantly share in the benefits? Look at the question too, on its philanthropic side. (We like to be benevolent when we can make something by it, you know.) What a boon to suffering humanity to develop this county, and

11

DESIGN No. 516.

BY THE CO-OPERATIVE BUILDING PLAN ASSOCIATION, ARCHITECTS.

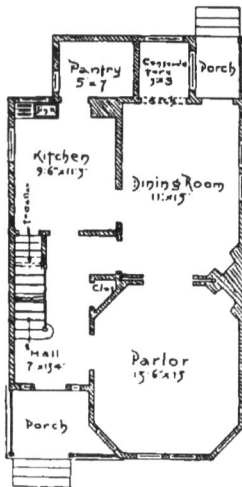

SIZE OF STRUCTURE—Front, 22 ft.; Side, 37 ft., 6 in.

ACCOMMODATIONS—Seven rooms, porch, hall, pantry, closets and cellar.

HEIGHT OF STORIES—Cellar, 7 ft.; First Story, 9 ft.; Second Story, 8 ft., 4 in.; Attic, 10 ft. in centre.

MATERIALS — Foundation, stone and brick walls; First Story, clap-boards; Second Story, shingles; Roof, shingles.

THE COST about $2,500. Further information concerning this design may be obtained free, by applying to the Co-operative Building Plan Association, Architects, 63 Broadway, New York.

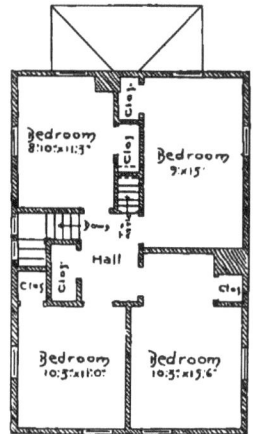

First Floor Plan.

Second Floor Plan.

give fathers and mothers and children a chance to escape the stuffy air, hot brick walls and pestilential emanations inseparable from crowded city life, to touch again the bosom of Mother Earth, and be rejuvenated and regenerated, *without materially increasing the cost of living.*

Very truly yours,

H. H. DALE.

———

You see that my friend's letter makes reference to the very liberal inducements offered by the Western Maryland Company to persons minded to settle anywhere on its line between Oakland, six miles from Baltimore, and Finksburgh, twenty-four miles; or, between Oakland and Greenmount, thirty-one miles, on the Baltimore & Harrisburg Division.

Such new settlers are given "a rebate of one-half the usual tariff rates on building materials used in new dwellings erected within one-half mile of any station between and including above points," and "a free pass between their station and Baltimore for one year for each $1000 expended in a new dwelling, up to $5000." (See page 37 for Inducements offered New Settlers.) So just make known to the Company your purpose to build a cottage costing, say $5000, comply with its regulations, and on its completion you will be entitled to a five years'

FREE RIDE

over the road between your home and Baltimore, beside a discount of one-half the cost of conveyance of building material. Do you want anything handsomer than that, my dear fellow? You can get commutation tickets through any ticket agent, and school tickets for the use of your children going to school.

Well, I have made this letter as full, and perhaps fuller, than you will have patience to read, so will bring it to an end, lest I bore you beyond the verge of your forbearance.

Yours cordially,

A. P. PENROSE.

———

PIMLICO, Md., July 17th, 1888.

—————, Esq.

You are kind enough to say, my dear fellow, that these rough and ready jottings of mine will be of use to you, so I continue them without further excuse.

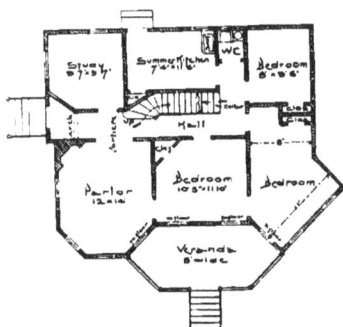

First Floor Plan.

Second Floor Plan.

DESIGN No. 438.

BY THE CO-OPERATIVE BUILDING PLAN ASSOCIATION, ARCHITECTS.

SIZE OF STRUCTURE—Front, 38 ft.; Side, including front veranda, 33 ft.

ACCOMMODATIONS—Twelve rooms, also veranda, balcony, closets, etc.

HEIGHT OF STORIES—Cellar, 6 ft., 8 in.; First Story, 9 ft.; Second Story, 8 ft., 8 in.

MATERIALS—Foundation, stone wall and brick piers; First Story, clap-boards; Second story, shingles; Gables, shingles; Roof, shingles.

SPECIAL FEATURES—Designed for erection in the Chautauqua Assembly Grounds, New York, near a hotel which is relied upon to supply meals. A small kitchen is provided as a resource in case of necessity. Nine bedrooms on the first and second floors; three more can be finished in the attic. Cellar under the parlor, enclosed with stone walls; remainder of the house is set on brick piers.

THE COST about $3,000. Further information concerning this design may be obtained free, by applying to the Co-operative Building Plan Association, Architects, 63 Broadway, New York.

From Arlington a branch road of a mile runs directly to Pimlico, where are held in their seasons the fairs of the Maryland Agricultural Society and the races of the Jockey Club. Anybody from a distance, as New York, or the East, may attend them without the least danger of a wet coat in case of rain, for he can, on arriving in Baltimore, step into a Western Maryland R. R. train under cover of Union station, and be set down at the grounds. Then, if he pleases, he can resume his journey on the same road and sojourn in the Blue Ridge, or make connections with other lines that will take him into southern or northeastern Pennsylvania, or southwesterly through the Shenandoah Valley, into the very heart of the South.

Indeed, no one can choose a more pleasant road over which to travel, if convenience, comfort and health be an object, to say nothing of the quest of beauty. From this point on to the grand climax of the mountains, scenery the most varied and lovely enchants the soul not too dull or dead to care for God's fair creation. A mile or two beyond the fine plateau occupied by the handsome grounds and buildings of Mt. Hope Retreat, brings us successively to the pleasant villages of Howardville and Pikesville, the well chosen location of some most elegant residences.

Toward Pikesville especially I felt a strong inclination, so bright, fresh and breezy in its surroundings, and then—only eleven miles from Baltimore. But how fast we fly in comparison with the speed of even a score of years ago! While I am still pondering, and holding the charms of Pikesville in my mind's eye, we overtake and leave in our rear, one after the other,

MT. WILSON AND McDONOGH,

the respective localities of two excellent charitable institutions, each named from its founder—the Thomas Wilson Sanitarium for the sick children of the poor, and the McDonogh Farm School for the education of poor boys. The site of the former was chosen by its trustees for its fine elevation, salubrious air, and abundant pure waters, after the examination and rejection of some 200 other sites proposed. The clear, bright stream of Gwynn's Falls flows through both places, a refreshing object to meet the eye, as the sun glances and dances over its surface.

At Green Spring Junction, fourteen miles from the city, the Western Maryland R. R. joins the Green Spring branch of the N. C. R. R., where mutual accommodations are interchanged in freight transfer. As we fly along, village follows village in quick succession, dotting the road on either side, environed

DESIGN No. 478.

BY THE CO-OPERATIVE BUILDING PLAN ASSOCIATION, ARCHITECTS.

First Floor Plan.

Second Floor Plan.

SIZE OF STRUCTURE — Front, 23 ft., 6 in.; Width over all, 42 ft.; Side not including rear veranda, 33 ft., 6 in.

ACCOMMODATIONS—Eight rooms, porch, rear veranda and balcony, cellar, closets, etc.

HEIGHT OF STORIES (measured in the clear)—Cellar, 6 ft., 6 in.; First Story, 9 ft.; Second Story, 8 ft.

MATERIALS—Foundation, 12-inch brick wall; First Story, clap-boards; Second Story, shingles; Roof, shingles.

THE COST about $3,000. Further information concerning this design may be obtained free, by applying to the Co-operative Building Plan Association, Architects, 63 Broadway, N. Y.

by fertile farms and dairy lands, whose products find a ready market at Baltimore and other places. Such a one is Owings' Mills, whose thrift is directed not alone to agriculture, and whose milling industries are carried forward by the busy bustling waters of Gwynn's Falls, as it courses on its rapid way through the village. Indeed, at close intervals all along this road I noted an abundance of

WATER-POWER,

not all of which has yet been utilized, as it may be, for purposes of manufacture.

Twenty miles from town and within a mile of the flourishing schools of St. George's Hall and Hannah More Academy, we come to Glyndon, a village of twenty years' growth, and still growing, a favorite resort of summer boarders, and a place that has charms for those who want a pretty country home within three-fourths of an hour of the city. This village is the railroad station of Reisterstown, half a mile away, on the Hanover and Westminster turnpike. Just beyond lies the spot where the Methodists of Baltimore hold their yearly camp-meetings, Emory Grove.

Here, having reached the junction point of the main line with the Baltimore & Harrisburg Division, I pause to give you and myself breathing time, and will explore the Division in another epistle.

Adieu till then, my friend.

A. P. Penrose.

Manchester, Md., July 20th, 1888.

——————, Esq.

Prompt as the tax-bill, my dear friend, behold my manuscript again, hoping, however, that you may not greet it with as wry a face as we sometimes wear on receipt of that irrepressible public document.

From Emory Grove the Baltimore & Harrisburg Division runs north and west, a distance of fifty-nine miles, to its terminus at Orrtana, Pennsylvania, just eight miles beyond Gettysburg. For some twelve miles from junction point it passes through a pleasant and fertile region, whose products of the farm and dairy find a shipping place at the charming little village stations that follow the road at intervals of not much more than a mile. The last of these, Greenmount, is the limit on the Division, fixed by the Western Maryland

First Floor Plan. Second Floor Plan.

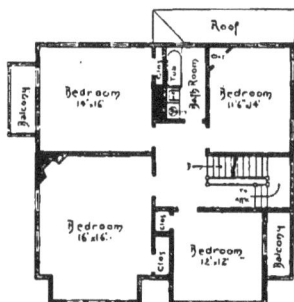

DESIGN No. 484.

BY THE CO-OPERATIVE BUILDING PLAN ASSOCIATION, ARCHITECTS.

SIZE OF STRUCTURE—Front, 36 ft. Side, 36 ft.

ACCOMMODATIONS—Ten large rooms, also porch, balcony, pantries, closets, bath and cellar.

HEIGHT OF STORIES—Cellar, 7 ft.; First Story, 9 ft., 6 in.; Second Story, 8 ft.; Attic, 8 ft.

MATERIALS—Foundation, stone walls; First Story, clap-boarded; Second Story, shingled; Roof, slate.

THE COST about $3,900. Further information concerning this design may be obtained free, by applying to the Co-operative Building Plan Association, Architects, 63 Broadway, N. Y.

Company in its provisions relating to settlers along its lines. Greenmount is connected, by a turnpike of two miles' length, with the considerable town of Manchester, which has a population of little less than a thousand, and paved and lighted streets.

Manchester stands at an elevation of 900 feet, and affords a beautiful landscape, for miles around, of hills, valleys, and distant mountains. With the

BRACING AIRS

and pure waters which its fine elevation secures, the salubrity of this town cannot be questioned, and I do not wonder that Baltimoreans have made it popular as a summer resort. It is not far from the pleasant picnic grounds of Maple Grove, which attracts excursion parties to take their pleasure in a spot so agreeable to every sense. A mile farther we find Millers, whose pleasant and healthful location makes it, too, a favorite rural resort. A large paper mill in the neighborhood brings its products to Millers for shipment. There are numerous paper mills on Gunpowder Falls which resort, for a like purpose, to Alesia, a small but thrifty village two miles beyond Millers.

Well, three miles farther, about thirty-nine from Baltimore, and we are upon the border line of two States at Lineboro, the seat of many industries, and surrounded by one of the richest of farming regions. The next station, Intersection, finds us fairly crossed into Pennsylvania. Here the Division is joined by the Bachman Valley R. R., which runs six miles through a country rich in

IRON,

and terminates at Ebbvale. As we reach Summit, we find ourselves in a hilly region at the very top of the grade. This is the place of shipment for the railroad ties of the country around, and we are further reminded that we are now in an iron district by sight of an iron foundry at the next station, Glenville.

Passing several little villages, prettily situated amid a rolling country, in which dairying is a prominent industry, we come to Valley Junction, where the Division unites with Hanover Junction Branch, running six miles to Hanover Junction on the N. C. R. R. From Valley Junction, the Division, which has heretofore extended nearly due north for twenty-eight miles from Emory Grove, makes a bend westward, and seven miles farther, over a beautiful, undulating surface, dotted with pretty villages, brings us to the important city of

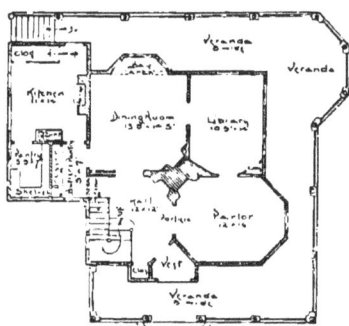

First Floor Plan. Second Floor Plan.

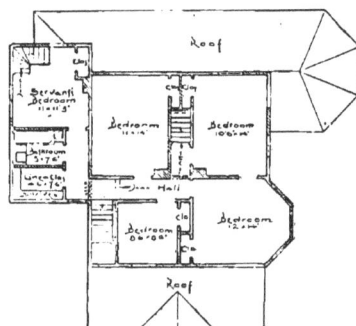

DESIGN No. 462.

BY THE CO-OPERATIVE BUILDING PLAN ASSOCIATION, ARCHITECTS.

SIZE OF STRUCTURE—Front, including kitchen and parlor bay, 41 ft.; Side, not including verandas, 31 ft., 6 in.

ACCOMMODATIONS—Eleven rooms, veranda, cellar, closets, bath, etc.

HEIGHT OF STORIES—Cellar, 6 ft., 6 in.; First Story, 9 ft., 6 in.; Second Story, 8 ft., 6 in.

MATERIALS—Foundation, stone walls; First Story, clap-boards; Second Story, shingles; Gables, shingles; Roof of house, slate; of verandas, shingles.

SPECIAL FEATURES—A compact arrangement of rooms. All the rooms of the first floor communicate. Direct access to the front hall from the kitchen without passing through a living room. Heater pipes and registers are provided in all the rooms. The attic is plastered and finished in one large play-room for children; three or four bedrooms can be made instead, if preferred. Cellar under the whole house.

THE COST about $5,000. Further information concerning this design may be obtained free, by applying to the Co-operative Building Plan Association, Architects, 63 Broadway, New York.

with its 4000 inhabitants, mostly people well-to-do, as the phrase goes. It is a veteran town of a hundred and fifty years and has its historic memories, having been the scene of a skirmish between the Union and Confederate forces two days prior to the battle of Gettysburg. It has an elevation of 600 feet, presents a neat appearance with its brick sidewalks and well-built houses, has all the appurtenances of a well-regulated city, and is the seat of large and varied industries.

Through several stations, chiefly important for lime shipments, we pass from Hanover to Berlin Junction, where this Division is met by the Berlin Branch R. R., which extends seven miles to East Berlin, its terminus, a prosperous and enterprising old town of 500 people, also passing on its way the fine, healthful town of Abbottstown. Through New Oxford, another of the many thrifty old towns of this line, over an elevated plain, and past Granite, the railroad station of Hunterstown, a short distance off the road, the pilgrim to historic shrines arrives at

GETTYSBURG,

forever memorable as the scene of one of the most decisive battles of the last war. It is nine miles north of the Maryland line, and stands upon a plain between two high ridges. The field of Gettysburg may be distinctly seen from a rift in the Blue Ridge Mountains at Monterey, two miles east of Pen-Mar, called, from that circumstance, Gettysburg Gap.

From Gettysburg eight miles to the small village of Orrtana, and we are at the present terminus of the Baltimore & Harrisburg Division. The face of the country throughout this Division retains the characteristic of the main line—elevation, which is but another term for healthfulness, signifying, as it does, pure air and water, while the scenery has all the pleasing variety to be found in a region of hills and undulating surface, side by side with the not less agreeable picture of human thrift.

Good bye, my friend. Now I face about again for the mountains of Maryland. Yours truly,

A. P. PENROSE.

MECHANICSTOWN, Md., July 22d, 1888.

————————, Esq.

You find me, my dear sir, resuming my journey again on the main line at Emory Grove. Through a beautiful rolling country diversified by hill

DESIGN No. 520.

BY THE CO-OPERATIVE BUILDING PLAN ASSOCIATION, ARCHITECTS.

First Floor Plan.

Second Floor Plan.

SIZE OF STRUCTURE—Front, 36 ft., 6 in., extreme width; Side, 51 ft.

ACCOMMODATIONS—Eleven rooms, veranda, halls, cellar, bath, closets, etc.

HEIGHT OF STORIES—Cellar, 6 ft., 6 in.; First Story, 9 ft., 6 in.; Second Story, 9 ft.; Third Story, 8 ft., 6 in.

MATERIALS — Foundation, brick and stone; First Story, clap-boards; Second Story, shingles; Gables, shingles; Roof, shingles.

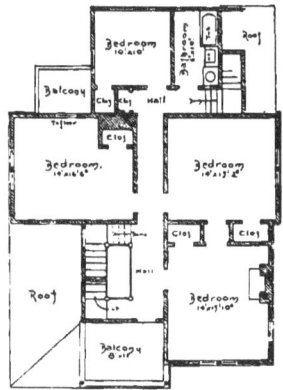

THE COST about $5,000. Further information concerning this design may be obtained free, by applying to the Co-operative Building Plan Association, Architects, 63 Broadway, N. Y.

22

and dale, passing Glen Morris and Glen Falls, whose suggestive names do not promise more than the beauty of their surroundings fulfill, I reach Finksburgh, a pleasant village on the Westminster turnpike, about a mile from the station, which, I bear in mind, is the limit of the Company's special favors to settlers on its main line. From here we speed on, touching the little village of Patapsco, the meeting point of two branches of the river whose name it bears; through the rich farm lands and pleasant hill slopes that surround the village of Carrollton; past busy Tannery, where the famous Schlosser sole leather is made, till we hail the city of

WESTMINSTER.

A thriving place is this, within an hour's reach of Baltimore and halfway to the Blue Ridge, blessed, by its mountain proximity, with cool nights in the hottest weather, and, of course, no mosquitoes, for it is lifted 726 feet above tide. An inviting place this to pitch one's tent indefinitely.

Between this town and the pretty summer resort of New Windsor and the salubrious little village of Linwood, is a tract containing large deposits of iron ore, which it might pay some enterprising capitalist to take in hand; and some day such a one will come forward. At Union Bridge is more mineral wealth, quarries of variegated marble, said to be equal to the best Tennessee. Near here was born the sculptor Rhinehart, and it was this marble that was the occasion of giving the happy turn to his genius, as he worked with a stone-cutter near his home.

At Frederick Junction this road unites with the Frederick Division of the Pennsylvania R. R., and five miles farther, at Rocky Ridge, junction is made with the Emmittsburg R. R., which thence runs north about seven miles to Emmittsburg.

From Rocky Ridge we behold the Blue Ridge clearly outlined, no longer shadowed by their crown of soft blue haze, but revealed in all their stately grace, reared above the hills that are gathered like trusting children about their feet. How beautiful are these tree-fringed mountains! lofty enough to carry the soul upward with the vision, out of the dust of commonplace things, yet near enough to Mother Earth to wear her colors and permit us the familiarities of kinship. The Blue Ridge is, I dare affirm, the loveliest of all the lovely Alleghany ranges. A trifle less lofty than the Alleghanies proper, what the mind loses in the sense of grandeur is gained in a humanizing delight in their

DESIGN No. 504.

BY THE CO-OPERATIVE BUILDING PLAN ASSOCIATION, ARCHITECTS.

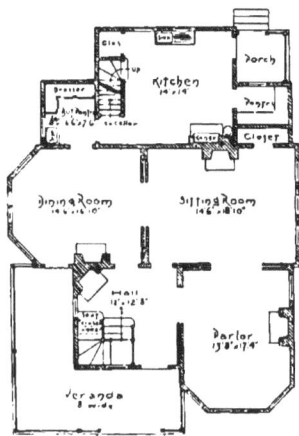

First Floor Plan.

SIZE OF STRUCTURE—Front, including veranda, 36 ft.; Side, 48 ft.

ACCOMMODATIONS—Ten rooms, veranda, balcony, halls, pantry, cellar, bath, closets, etc.

HEIGHT OF STORIES—Cellar, 7 ft.; First Story, 9 ft., 6 in.; Second Story, 9 ft.; Attic, 8 ft.

MATERIALS — Foundation, stone and brick; First Story, clapboarded; Second Story, shingled; Roof, slate.

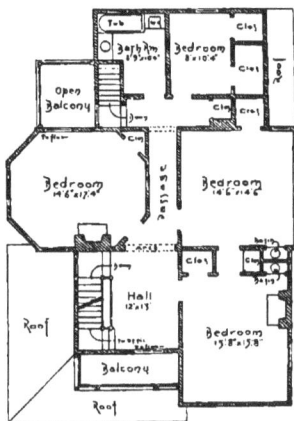

Second Floor Plan.

THE COST about $5,500. Further information concerning this design may be obtained free, by applying to the Co-operative Building Plan Association, Architects, 63 Broadway, N. Y.

and fraternization. One has no sense of solitude, monotony or peril, as the bald and towering peaks of the great Rocky ranges impress us, but only of Nature herself in her fairest, kindliest, friendliest aspect, breathing upon us her life-giving breath, inviting us to be healthy and happy. Like other children, I think I love my Mother Nature better when she is kind, tender and smiling, than when she is stern, forbidding and threatening.

Mechanicstown, a place of 1000 population, is the junction point of Monocacy Valley R. R., which runs to Catoctin Furnaces. Nature here wears a charming face, and my eyes were arrested by the fine picture presented in the Falls of Hunting Creek, which come dashing over the rocks and down the mountain side, flowing through the town that shelters itself at the mountain's foot. Then raise your eyes from its restless activity and fix them upon the tall, immovable Chimney Rock, and you see Nature at a glance in two contrasting shapes. When we reach Sabillasville we realize that we are indeed in

A MOUNTAIN REGION,

for here we cross South Mountain, and what a view opens before us! But lest I be tempted to afflict you, my friend, with efforts at description, I hurry on. Three miles more will bring us to the summit of the Blue Ridge at Monterey. But of this in another letter.

Yours fraternally,

A. P. PENROSE.

MONTEREY, Md., July 25th, 1888.

————————, Esq.

Here am I, sixty-nine miles from Baltimore, 1400 feet above sea level, on the summit of the Blue Ridge at Monterey. This is one of the chief summer resorts on the line, and here Monterey Hotel is located, on a cultivated plateau of 400 acres, one mile from where the railroad crosses the mountain summit. It is the descendant of an old log tavern that flourished over a hundred years ago, accommodating the health seekers of the sparse population of that day. The log tavern gave way to a frame boarding house, and this in turn to the present spacious structure, where 250 guests may be entertained, to whom, I warrant, this mountain air gives a keen appetite. The buildings are newly and thoroughly furnished, having baths, gas, bowling alley, and a detached play-room for children.

Side Elevation

DESIGN No. 485.

BY THE CO-OPERATIVE BUILDING PLAN ASSOCIA-
TION, ARCHITECTS.

First Floor Plan.

Second Floor Plan.

SIZE OF STRUCTURE—Front, not including veranda, 38 ft., 6 in.; Width over all, 67 ft.; Side, including veranda, 59 ft.

ACCOMMODATIONS—Seventeen rooms, also verandas, balconies, halls, pantries, closets and all modern improvements.

HEIGHT OF STORIES (measured in the clear)—Cellar, 8 ft.; First Story, 10 ft., 6 in.; Second Story, 9 ft., 6 in.; Attic, 8 ft., 6 in.

MATERIALS—Foundation, brick walls; First Story, clap-boards; Second Story, shingles; Roof, shingles.

SPECIAL FEATURES—Cellar with cemented bottom under the whole house. Laundry, with a set of three tubs under the kitchen. Double sliding doors connect the principal rooms. The interior finish throughout is of pine or whitewood stained. Staircase is of hard wood.

THE COST about $9,000. Further information concerning this design may be obtained free, by applying to the Co-operative Building Plan Association, Architects, 63 Broadway, New York.

Among the distinguishing features of this mountain region are the good roads and beautiful drives, which abound with every variety of scenery. Emmittsburg, Gettysburg, Antietam, Mont Alto and Doubling Gap are from nine to twenty miles distant on macadamized roads; and there are innumerable shorter drives on dirt roads, of two to six miles, among them drives to Mount Quirauk, High Rock, Blue Mountain House and other places. Points to the southwest, as Harper's Ferry, Luray and others, have been brought very near, in time, since the building of the Shenandoah Valley R. R. between Hagerstown and Roanoke, the junction with the Norfolk & Western R. R.

The remarkable salubrity of the air, the entire exemption from malaria, and the

PURITY OF THE WATERS

from wells and natural springs, have been among the chief attractions of Monterey from the earliest settlement of the country, especially in lung and throat troubles and general debility. Children suffering from summer complaints seldom fail to be relieved when taken to the bracing mountain air of Monterey. Rocky Spring, Bubbling Spring and Gum Spring are within easy walking distance, and the mountain peaks of Lone Pine, Monterey and Wild Cat are within a few hundred yards of the hotel. Their summits are from 1600 to 2000 feet above tide level, and overlook the picturesque Cumberland Valley as far as the eye can reach to the north and southwest; while to the east the battle-field of Gettysburg, only fourteen miles distant, is plainly spread out below, with the valley of the Monocacy stretching southward to the Potomac.

As Monterey is situated on a plateau on the summit of the Blue Ridge Mountains, there are

MAGNIFICENT VIEWS

in every direction, and the conformation of the ground is such that from the neighboring mountain peaks there is always an air blowing. This fact led the hotel company to purchase the surrounding 300 acres of land, and have it divided into building lots by C. H. Latrobe, C. E., of Baltimore. These lots are now for sale, and a mountain health-city is springing up here, as the advantages are unsurpassed, and express trains make the distance to Baltimore in only two and a quarter hours.

Already, Francis T. King, Martin Hawley, Dr. James Carey Thomas, Captain Norwood and Dr. Elias C. Price, of Baltimore, and Captain Taylor

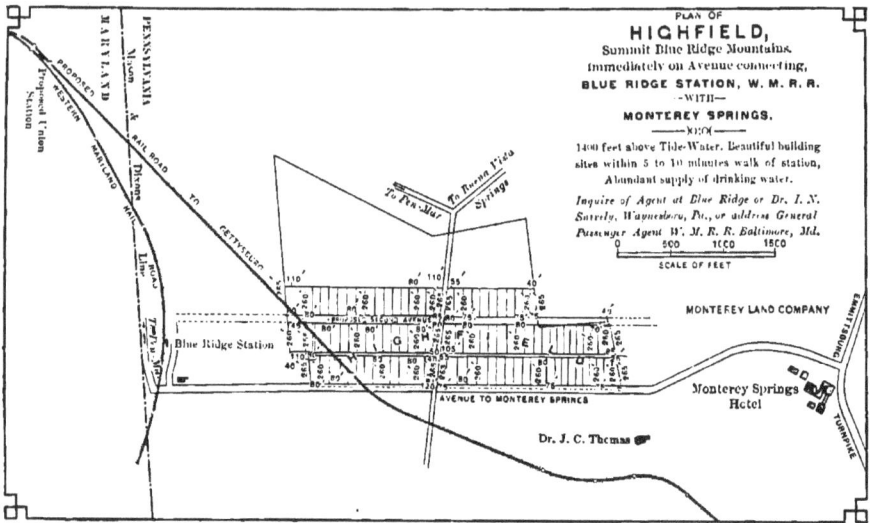

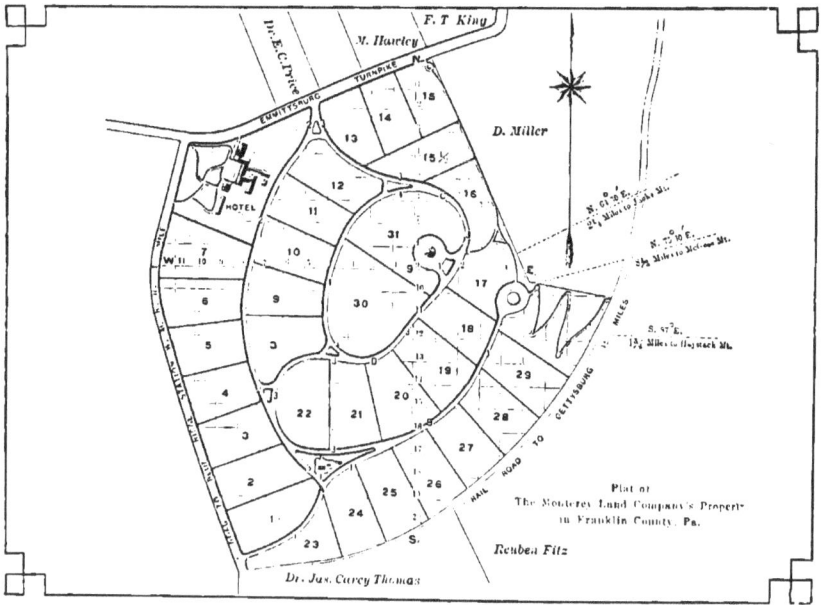

and Colonel Page, of Norfolk, have built beautiful cottages, and several others contemplate doing so at an early day.

The advantages of these sites are that families can lodge in their cottages and get their meals at the hotel; or they can keep house, and obtain regular supplies of meat, vegetables and fruit in the neighborhood from wagons which call daily. The lots are laid off so that each one has a fine view, and the best of water and drainage. Reliable builders and contractors in Hagerstown and Waynesboro are prepared to erect cottages upon very reasonable terms. As the property is all in the hands of men of means and enterprise, there will no doubt soon be a mountain city at Monterey.

Applications can be made to John Curlett, President of Maryland White Lead Works, 37 Post Office Avenue, Baltimore.

So, with the lungs invigorated by the bracing air of a high altitude, beyond the reach of malarious gases and foul odors, the digestion thereby quickened, and the body recuperated by sound sleep, such as they only can know who breathe an air like this, none but the incorrigible can help growing healthy, handsome and good-humored. It is this surely which accounts for the proverbial healthfulness of mountain dwellers.

· A SUMMER HOME

in such a spot would exactly meet the wants of a man like you, for example, who must not leave his business for a protracted season, and can not afford to send his family to an expensive watering place or rural boarding house, while he keeps a dismal bachelor's hall in the hot city. What rustication is equal to that enjoyed in the independence of one's own home?

Yours sincerely,

A. P. PENROSE.

EDGEMONT, Md., July 26th, 1888.

——————, Esq.

Since my last greeting, my dear fellow, I have whirled through Pen-Mar and looked down upon a magnificent world, like an alien from another planet, from the dizzy height of High Rock. As it is futile to attempt a description of the indescribable, I will say no more of these spots.

Behold me, then, at Blue Mountain, at your service. Leading from here to High Rock and Pen-Mar are fine carriage and foot roads, made and kept

DESIGN No. 499.

BY THE CO-OPERATIVE BUILDING PLAN ASSOCIATION, ARCHITECTS.

SIZE OF STRUCTURE—Front, not including carriage porch, 42 ft.; Side, including front veranda, 68 ft.

ACCOMMODATIONS—Fourteen rooms, veranda, halls, pantries, closets, bath, etc.

HEIGHT OF STORIES—Cellar, 8 ft.; First Story, 9 ft., 6 in.; Second Story, 8 ft., 6 in.; Attic, 8 ft., 6 in.

MATERIALS—Foundation, stone walls; First Story, clap-boarded; Second Story, shingled; Gables, cemented in panels; Roofs, slate, with terra cotta crestings and finials.

First Floor Plan.

Second Floor Plan.

SPECIAL FEATURES—Cellar under the whole house. A billiard room, 14x18 ft., is finished underneath the back parlor. Sliding doors on first floor, hung from the top. Large stained glass windows over the staircase. Electric bells and annunciators.

THE COST about $9,000. Further information concerning this design may be obtained free, by applying to the Co-operative Building Plan Association, Architects, 63 Broadway, N. Y.

in order by the railroad company. The Blue Mountain House is a fine structure, with all the appliances of the complete modern city hotel, set amid the rugged mountains, differing only in the advantageous particular of having made width supply the need of height, so that though but three stories high, it is capacious enough to entertain 400 guests. It is girt with piazzas, and as you look down from them upon the Cumberland and Shenandoah Valleys, guarded round about by mountains, stretching as far as the eye can range, you feel as if you had the world before you—a large piece of it certainly.

Besides Baltimore, this house is in such

CLOSE PROXIMITY TO THE LARGE CITIES

of New York, Philadelphia, Washington, Richmond and others, that it is accessible to any in two and a half to eight hours. At Hagerstown connection may be made with the Cumberland Valley R. R. from Harrisburg, or with the Shenandoah Valley R. R. from the south; thus, passengers may reach Blue Mountain with but one change of cars.

Three miles beyond Blue Mountain is Edgemont, a small and new place, named from its location on the edge of South Mountain. Here is a

FINE FRUIT-GROWING TRACT,

whose grapes and peaches, from their superior quality, command the highest prices in Eastern markets, whither they have ready access. This locality has made wonderful advances in peach-growing within a few years, the soil having been found remarkably adapted to their cultivation. Market facilities are excellent and farms are cheap, those within five miles of Hagerstown bringing sixty to ninety dollars per acre, and those more remote half that price. I hear that not infrequently owners are able to pay for their farms from the profits of one year's crop, and that $15,000 to $20,000 have been netted from a single farm.

If this is so, the sooner you and I become peach growers, the better for our pockets. Come, suppose we go into partnership for a peach farm, and combine the delights of these surroundings with the conveniences of the city, to which we are but

THREE HOURS DISTANT.

I was told that whereas, in other localities, the bearing time of a peach tree is limited to about three years, here on the west slope of the Blue Ridge trees retain their vigor and are profitably fruitful even when planted thirty years,

DESIGN No. 471.

BY THE CO-OPERATIVE BUILDING PLAN ASSOCIATION ARCHITECTS.

SIZE OF STRUCTURE—Front, including veranda, 48 ft.; Side, 78 ft.

ACCOMMODATIONS—Fifteen rooms, also verandas, balconies, pantries, closets, bath and all modern appliances.

HEIGHT OF STORIES—First Story, 10 ft., 6 in.; Second Story, 9 ft., 6 in.; Third Story, 8 ft.

MATERIALS—Foundation, stone or brick piers; First Story, clap-boards; Second Story, shingles; Gables, shingles; Roof, shingles.

SPECIAL FEATURES—A hall, ten feet wide, runs through the house from front to rear, in the central part of which is a recess for the stairway; also, a platform the length of this recess and projecting into the hall. This platform is raised two steps above the floor of the hall, and from it the stairway starts. The ceilings of the hall and the dining room show the timbers, and are paneled with red baywood, or what is commonly known as and passes for mahogany. The wainscoting and trimming throughout the first story are of the same wood; trimming elsewhere is yellow pine. In the attic, besides the large hallway, there is a billiard room, 14 ft. x 22 ft., two large bed rooms and a tank room. No cellar. This house was designed for and built in the South, where cellars are seldom required. A cellar under the whole house, with stone or brick walls, would cost $450 additional.

THE COST about $10,000. Further information concerning this design may be obtained free, by applying to the Co-operative Building Plan Association, Architects, 63 Broadway, N. Y.

obviating the necessity for the annual planting of orchards to replace those worn out.

Think all this over, my friend, and let us talk about it when we meet.

Yours heartily,

A. P. PENROSE.

SHIPPENSBURG, Pa., July 28th, 1888.

————————, Esq.

This, I think, my dear sir, is the appropriate place to sketch my trip over the Baltimore & Cumberland Valley R. R., which joins the main line of the Western Maryland R. R. at Edgemont, where you last heard from me. From this point it runs northward thirty-four miles and terminates at Shippensburg, Pa. Several miles through a rich farming country bring us to the large and thriving town of

WAYNESBORO.

This is the centre of a large grain-growing region, and an elevator has been built by the railroad company to meet the necessity for handling the grain for the market. Waynesboro is in an elevated situation, has an enterprising population of 4000, and is the seat of a large amount of manufacturing. Through a fertile country, strewn with villages, fifteen miles beyond, we find historic

CHAMBERSBURG,

memorable for the disasters that befell it at the hands of an invading army. It has many fine buildings and extensive and varied industries.

It is but twelve miles farther to the terminus of this road and its junction with the Harrisburg & Potomac R. R. at

SHIPPENSBURG.

This is an old town, known to the days prior to the Revolution. I think we read of it when we were boys, in connection with the French and Indian war. Its population of 3000 is well supplied with everything essential to their moral, mental and material welfare.

If you are getting weary of my scribblings, my dear fellow, as by this time you have a right to be, you will be relieved to know that the next will be my final letter, in which I shall carry my observations to the end of the main road. Can't you run up here for a day or so and rusticate a little with me?

Yours expectantly,

A. P. PENROSE.

——————, Esq.

Well! here I am again at Edgemont, and on to picturesque Smithsburg. But as I write with practical intent, I will only note of it that here wood, lumber, and building material of all kinds may be had cheap, because of the town's nearness to the mountain. Nor, as I run through Cavetown, just beyond, will I say anything of its wonderfully interesting cave, except barely to make known to you the fact of its existence; for I am in a hurry to push on to Hagerstown, toward my journey's end.

Hagerstown numbers 10,000 population, and is rapidly growing, having doubled within the last ten years, owing, no doubt, to her excellent railroad facilities. A practical sign that she is resolved to go ahead is that one of her real estate firms offers to donate ground near the railways, for manufacturing enterprises,

FREE OF CHARGE.

The advantages to manufacturing establishments that may locate here or elsewhere along the line of the Western Maryland R. R., are numerous. They secure a healthful, eligible site, within a short distance of Baltimore markets, which ensures them regular mail communication, cheap living, fuel and labor; for Baltimore is noted as being the place where one can live best at least cost, of any large city in the Union. All such settlers have the benefit of the

SAME THROUGH RATES

to principal points South and West that apply to Baltimore itself, these being less than those of Philadelphia and New York.

But the world moves and so must we; so good-bye, Hagerstown. Six miles ahead, ninety-three from Baltimore, we enter the century-old town of Williamsport. Here terminates the Western Maryland Main Line, and its completion to this point, opening up to the town markets at Baltimore and other places, has given a push to industries that else had never been. Here is a prodigious amount of

WATER-POWER,

much of which has been availed of, but more is awaiting the hand of enterprise.

To a beautiful scenery of plain, mountain and water, is added a generous climate, and the town and its neighborhood are proverbial for the health and longevity of the people. Property is low; there is no mania for artificial or speculative values. Town lots, unimproved, sell for $25 to $600, each containing about one-third of an acre, and rate according to location. Substantially improved property can be had very low.

Considering the fertility of the surrounding country; the finely improved farms, rating from $40 to $100 per acre, according to location and improvements; the advantage of cheap merchandise and corresponding good prices of grain, hay, produce, manufactures, etc., by reason of low and competing rail and water transportation; it seems also one of the most desirable of places for those seeking good farms and

LOCATIONS FOR MANUFACTURING

and business. With its rich country around, great water-power, cheap fuel and transportation, Williamsport has been repeatedly referred to as the future Manchester of Western Maryland.

Now, my friend, you have the benefit of my observations during my late trip, and perhaps you may, as I hope to do, reap something therefrom of practical good to both of us. I do not hesitate to say that no road leading out of Baltimore presents to the settler more

ADVANTAGES

than the Western Maryland, whether we consider the beauty of scenery, or the fine elevation of its whole line, taking one out of the lurking places of miasmatic vapors and contaminated waters into the highlands of health, or the convenience of nearness to Baltimore, coupled with the best of terminal facilities and frequent trains, or, finally, the special inducements offered by the road itself and by the busy enterprise of the country through which it passes.

Yours faithfully,

A. P. PENROSE.

Extract from "BALTIMORE SUN,"

Saturday, July 21, 1888.

Among the noticeable features of travel by the Western Maryland Railroad is the suddenness of the change from city to country. The train, after leaving Fulton Avenue Station, passes through a deep cut for several hundred feet and then plunges into the midst of lovely scenery, with none of the usual detractions of town-lot outskirts.

The train gradually climbs up the long slope extending from tide-level to the top of the mountains, and when Arlington is reached, only seven miles from the city, the passenger is 400 feet above tide-water. Moving on with a steadily pulling motion one is whirled past cool farm houses appearing through the thick shade trees, smoothly mown fields dotted with the standing shocks of wheat waiting for the thrasher, green pastures, with the cattle lazily grazing, and a beautiful country on both sides. The land is not too hilly for improved agricultural implements, nor so level as to require extensive drainage. It is gently rolling, with wide level stretches and a good farming country.

Mount Hope and Mount Wilson, only four miles apart, are both located in this healthful section, the former being one of the best equipped and managed institutions for the insane, and the latter a sanitarium for children. Just one mile beyond Mount Wilson is the McDonogh School. These three institutions were placed in this country on account of its elevation. pure water, natural forest and easy accessibility by steam. Through the McDonogh farm of over eight hundred acres flows Gwynn's Falls, discharging several million gallons of pure water over its gravelly bottom every day. In the country around the farmers live in substantial houses, which are often built of stone, and the yard and lots are inclosed by stone walls. Nearly all have ice-houses.

So beautiful is the country, so cool and pleasant the place, than many from the city who like to spend a quiet life during the hot season come out and board in the farm houses. Its natural advantages of water, forest and fresh air, and its accessibility by steam road brought the large camp-meetings to this part of the country. After passing by Green Spring Junction and Owings' Mill the camp-meeting grounds of the African Methodist Church are reached, and a few miles further beyond St. George's, Glyndon and Reisterstown lie the Emory Grove camp-meeting grounds of the Methodists of Baltimore. This site, in a finely-wooded and watered locality, was chosen after some months of careful search. The houses and tents are put up in the forest with scarcely the undergrowth cut down, and many persons live there not only during the camp, but for the summer. Thousands are brought to the regular services by special excursion trains.

Moving by Glen Morris, Glen Falls, Finksburg, Tank, Patapsco, Carrollton, the stations of Tannery and Westminster, within three miles of each other, are reached. The former is the seat of a large tanning establishment, and the latter is situated a thousand feet above tide-water and on top of a narrow ridge dividing the drainage of the Potomac from the Patapsco.

After passing Quarry, Avondale, Medford, Wakefield, New Windsor and Linwood, the traveler reaches Union Bridge, with quarries of the finest marble near by. It is famous as the birthplace of one of the greatest sculptors of America, W. H. Rhinehart, who was born and reared on his father's farm within a short distance of this station.

The country now becomes much more broken, and the views from some high trestle or the side of a steep hill are more extended. The gently-sloping fields of grain and corn and the green pastures give way in part to steep, rocky hillsides and narrow, dark valleys. The large trees of the natural forest are interspersed and replaced by mountain fir and spruce pine. The round hills yield to sharp ones, in places rough and rocky. The road is more tortuous and winding, the curves are sharper, and the rate of the train is very much slower. The high, steep hills and the beds of bare rock make this section on up into the higher parts an attractive study for the geologist.

Climbing by Middleburg, Frederick Junction, York Road. Double Pipe Creek, Rocky Ridge, Loys, Graceham, Mechanicstown, Catoctin Furnace, Deerfield and Sabillasville, Monterey, on the summit of the mountains, is finally reached. General's Lee's army encamped here the first night after the battle of Gettysburg. Monterey is connected by macadamized roads with Emmittsburg, Gettysburg, Antietam and other places. The advantages of this locality for pleasant summer homes have been realized by many prominent men in Baltimore, and many houses have been built, and beautiful grounds and drives laid out.

Just a few miles from the top of the mountain is the "Horse Shoe Curve." Its elevation and the curious upheavals and distortions of the rock have made it a favorite field of investigation for geologists, and the rare plants found here have attracted the attention of eminent botanists. Near by, the Devil's Race-course, a vast bed of rock broken into thousands of pieces and resembling an exaggerated cobble-stone pavement, occupies the surface of a long, shallow depression, more than a mile in length, and hidden away in the midst of woods.

A few miles further are Pen-Mar and Blue Mountain, commanding one of the finest views to be had in this country. Spread out like a vast panorama before him, one can see, stretching away far beneath him, a level expanse of country, smiling with peace and plenty. The hard, white roads, crossing in every direction, fade away into mere threads in the distance. Relieving the expanse of green surface, the white farm houses nestle among the green waving branches of the shade trees. Small clusters of houses tell of prosperous little villages in this rich valley. Afar off through a gap in the mountains can be seen historic Gettysburg, almost like a speck, and the route of the invading army from the South is pointed out.

Beyond Pen-Mar are Edgemont, Smithburg and Cavetown, the last receiving its name from the cave within a few hundred feet of the railroad station. It is not known how far some of the chambers of the cave extend, as no one has been bold enough to explore the ice-cold recesses. Chewsville, Antietam and Hagerstown, the last in the midst of a most flourishing farming country, and Williamsport, which was made historic by the crossing and re-crossing of the opposing armies during the civil war, are terminal points of interest.

Western + Maryland + Railroad + Co.

INDUCEMENTS TO NEW SETTLERS.

REGULATIONS UNDER WHICH OFFERED.

IN EFFECT JANUARY 1, 1888.

RESOLUTION OF BOARD OF DIRECTORS.

RESOLVED, "That the President be authorized to put in effect the plan of inducing new settlers upon the line of road between Oakland (6 miles) and Finksburg (24 miles from Baltimore), by giving a rebate of one-half the usual tariff rates on building materials used in new dwellings erected within one-half mile of any station between and including the above points, and by issuing to all such new settlers erecting dwellings as above, a free pass between their station and Baltimore for one year for each $1000 expended in a new dwelling, up to $5000."

Under the above the following regulations have been adopted :

1. New settlers desiring to avail of these inducements must, before commencing work, make application to the Railroad Company upon the proper printed form, stating fully the location of their proposed new dwellings, their estimated cost (not including the land), the points from which the building material will be shipped, and if intended to be occupied in each case as a residence by the builder.

2. All arrangements must be concluded between the Company and the party making the improvement before the erection of the dwelling.

3. All building material should be invariably consigned to the party who has arranged with the Company and not to the contractors, as several of the latter may be engaged upon the same improvement, or the same contractor may be engaged upon other work upon the line of the road.

4. Upon the completion of the dwelling ready for occupancy, a certificate of cost, not including land, must be made to the Railroad Company upon the proper printed form.

5. Upon a compliance with the above regulations, by those whose applications have been accepted, and presentation to the Railroad Company of receipted freight bills, a rebate of one-half of the amount of this Company's freight—paid at regular tariff rates—will be allowed, less 2 cents per 100 pounds, the Tunnel charge, when from stations in Baltimore east of Fulton, and a pass between Baltimore and the station at or near which the improvement is located, will be issued for one year for each $1000 expended as above ; but in no case will a pass be issued to any one individual for more than five years. These passes will expire with the calendar year, unless otherwise limited, and are renewable until the expiration of the period above indicated.

6. Printed forms of application and certificate will be furnished by the Company.

7. Until further notice, the scope of this arrangement will be extended to include those erecting buildings to be rented to and occupied by new residents, not including transient summer renters, but only those who purpose making their home upon the line of the road. In such cases passes will be issued which will not be renewable during the time that the houses are unoccupied, nor after the expiration of the term (one year's travel for each $1000 expended, dating from first issue of pass), even though this privilege may not have been continuously enjoyed, owing to the house being unoccupied.

8. The term for which pass will be issued will begin with the completion of the dwelling.

9. The above arrangement is hereby extended to apply to stations on the Baltimore & Harrisburg Division, between Greenmount and Emory Grove inclusive, the tickets given in this connection to apply to travel between such B. & H. Division stations and Baltimore.

B. H. GRISWOLD,
General Freight and Passenger Agent.

J. M. HOOD,
General Manager.

STATION	OWNER	ADDRESS	BY ACRE OR LOT. NUMBER OF ACRES OR SIZE OF LOT.	BY TURNPIKE OR ROAD.	SELLING PRICE, ACRE OR LOT.	DISTANCE FROM STATION.	If House for sale or rent; price if for sale; rent per year.	No. of R'ms	No. of stories
OAKLAND	Newman Estate	Oakland, Md.	By acre. 40 acres	By both	$1,000 per acre	At station	Six houses, $300 to $400 rent.	10	2–3
"	Lewis V. Wise	"	50 acres	Both	$1,000 per acre	50 yds.	Cottage $300, for rent.	8	2
"	J. Henschel	"	0 acres	Turnpike	$1,000 per acre	1/2 mile	House $450, for rent.	12	3
"	C. J. Hull	"	50 acres in lots 50 x 100 feet.	Both	$50 to $200 per lot	1/2 mile	3 houses	8	3
"	D. C. G. Hill	"	5 acres. Lots 1/4 acre	"	By lot, $500	1/2 mile			
ARLINGTON	Thos. J. Haywood	Arlington, Md	60 acres	Both	$600 per acre	1/4 mile	House and stable, rent $600.	15	3
"	O. L. Rogers	"	5 acre lots	"	$8,000 per lot	1/4 mile	Cottage for sale.	10	2
"	Mrs. Dr. Allen	"	By lots. 3 acres	Turnpike	For rent, $250 per year	1/2 mile	Cottage for rent with land, $250.	8	2
"	Mrs. Shirlock	"	16 acres by acre or lot.	"	$400 per acre	1 mile	None.		
"	Dr. W. H. Hoops	"	15 acres	"	Rent $600 per year.	1/2 mile	Cottage and lot, rent $600.	12	3
"	Dr. W. H. Hoops	"	40 acres	"	Rent $1,000.	1/2 mile	Hotel or boarding h'se, $1,000 rent, with land.	20	3
"	Dr. W. H. Hoops	"	25 acres. Acre or lot.	County road	Selling price, $1,000 per acre.	1 mile	Cottage and stable for rent.	10	2
MT. WILSON	W. Ferguson	209 Clay St., Balt.	House and 4 acres of land	County road		300 yds.	For sale	16	3
GREEN SPRING JUNC	J. H. Snyder	Green Ridge	About 6 acres, with paper mill.	County road	Cannot give price.	1/4 mile			
OWINGS' MILLS	J. C. Shugard	Owings' Mills	18 or 19 acres, will sell in lots from 1 to 6.	Fronting on turnpike.	Whole place $9,000	300 yds.		13	3
TIMBER GROVE	Dr. J. J. Krozier	Timber Grove	40 acres	On Railroad	Fine fruit, handsome improvements, will sell for $17,000.	At station	Large residence	12	3
ST. GEORGE'S	Thos. Fairley	St. George's	In lots. Lots any size desired	County road	$50 lease or $500 in fee per foot.	100 yds. in			
FINKSBURG	C. Buckley	Finksburg	By acre. 300 acres	By turnpike	$40 per acre	2 miles			
"	L. H. Stocksdale	"	100 acres from $40 to $60 per acre	County road	$40 to $60 per acre	2 1/2 miles			
"	E. N. Buckingham	"	100 acres	By turnpike	$40 to $60 per acre	2 miles			
PATAPSCO STATION	W. H. Westaway	Patapsco Sta.	100 acres	County road	$50 per acre	1/4 mile	House for sale.	8	2
"	Wm. L. Richards	"	1 acre	"	$500.	At station	House for sale	4	2
"	J. H. Chew	"	14 acres	"	$3,000 per lot	300 yds.	House for sale	8	4
"	Wm. L. Richards	"	1/2 acre	"	$300 per lot	At station	House for sale	3	1 1/2
"	G. W. Weaver	"	68 acres	"	$3,000 per acre	1/4 mile	House for sale.	6	2
"	J. H. Chew	"	4 acres	"	$400 per lot	1/4 mile	House for sale.	8	3
WESTMINSTER	C. E. Fink	Westminster	13 acres, in quantity to suit buyer	Fronting on 2 streets	$150 per acre or $50 to $200 per lot.	400 yds	House and barn included in price, water all through house.	10	2
"	M. J. & F. C. Lynch	"	56 acres	Bond street	$8,000 to $9,000 for whole or $150 to $175 per acre.	600 yds.			
"	Dr. J. H. Billingslea	"	House and lot	Pennsylvania avenue	$2,300 for all	4 blocks	For sale: price given	7, hall	2
"	Miss C. Hardy	"	House and lot 102 feet front	"	$1,200.	5 blocks	H'se & ground for sale	6	2
"	Heirs of Mrs. J. Smith	"	House and lot 120 feet front	248 East Main Street	$4,000.	1/2 mile	House and lot for sale. Stable, lovely home.	4	2 1/2

Location	Owner	P.O.	Description	Road	Price	Distance	Buildings / Remarks		
WESTMINSTER	G. W. Mathews	Westminster	By acre. 59 acres in farm	1½ miles from Wakefield, 4 miles from Westminster.	$3,500 for all	Given	Brick house for sale, included in price of farm.	8	2
MEDFORD	J. W. Pennington	Medford	130 acres and house	County road	$50 per acre	1½ miles		9	2
LOYS	S. J. Beiler	Loys	160 acres	County road	$35 per acre	¾ mile		8	2
BLUE RIDGE SUMMIT	R. O. Willard	Blue Ridge Summit	House and 2 acres	County road	Per acre $100 to $300.	1200 feet	2 houses for sale $2,000	7	2
"	Bischhoff & Kimmel	"	25 acres and 125 acres	"		2 miles	1 house for sale or rent.	11	2
"	S. Dewees	"	20 acres	"		½ mile	1 house for sale, $900.	4	2
PEN-MAR	Rouzer & Shover	Pen-Mar	3 acres, house, warehouse, etc.	County road				8	1½
EDGEMONT	J. Stouffer	Edgemont	13 acres wooded land	Mountain road	$50 per acre	¾ mile			
HAGERSTOWN	Mrs. J. B. Emmert	Hagerstown	61 acres	Turnpike road	$100 per acre	½ mile from Chewsville.		8	2
WILLIAMSPORT	Chas. Hodimyer / V. Cushwa	Williamsport	40 acres. Will sell in whole or in lots. 25 or 30 acres	Turnpike and public road.		At station / At station		4	2
FAIRVIEW	W. S. Star	Boring, P.O., Md	House and ¼ acre lot	County road		300 yds		4	2½
ARCADIA	A. H. Cole / Mrs. A. Burke / Richard H. Gill	Upperco, P.O., Md	Farm—100 acres—so much per acre	On Pike at R.R. Sta.	$50 to $150 per acre	100 yds	House for rent, $60 per year; selling price $750.	5	
LINEBORO	J. A. Tracy	Lineboro	101 acres—farm	County road	$40 per acre	2 miles	For sale	7	2
"	A. D. Wentz	"	¼ acre house and lot	"	$1,000	At station	For sale	8	2
"	Ed. Sandruck	"	House and lot—¼ acre	"	$600	At station	For sale or rent	4	1
"	R. H. Swanned	"	House and lot—3 acres	"	$1,200	1½ miles	For sale or rent	7	2
HANOVER	Mrs. Mary Thomas	Hanover, Pa	House and lot—lot 30 x 100 feet	County road	House and lot, $1,000.	100 yds		7	2
GRANITE	J. A. Stallsmit	Granite	16 acres, large warehouse, hay shed, good stables all in good order.	500 yards of turnpike and a good county road to the door.	$6,000; 2 good wells of water.	At station. P. O. in build'g		8	2
GETTYSBURG	H. A. Scott	Gettysburg	7½ acres adjoining National Cemetery	3 roads or paved sts	$7,000, or the houses and 1 acre $5,500.	3,600 feet	2 houses—$7,000; with out land $5,500.	33	3
GEISER	R. Plosser	Waynesboro	House and 228 acres farm	County road	$40 per acre	1 mile		9	2
WAYNESBORO	J. M. Epple	Waynesboro	5 vacant lots	Lutersburg street	$200 per lot	100 yds	7 houses, $2,000 selling price; $120 rent p'r yr.	7	2
CHAMBERSBURG	J. W. Heimbird	Cumberland	40 acres farm land 75 lots 324, 200 feet	2 county roads	$100 an acre; per lot $75 to $200.	per lot 500 yds	Some houses for sale or rent.		
SHIPPENSBURG	Jno. and Mrs. Yundt	Shippensburg	House and 187 acres by acre	County road	Reasonable	2 miles	1 brick house for sale.	8	2
"	Heirs of J. D. Geesaman	"	Town lot 113 ft. front, 256 ft. d'p, b'se with large b'k b'd'g, gas, water, lawn, fruit.	Main street	Lot, house, complete, $5,000.	100 yds	2 stores of same.	6, 8, hall	2, 2
MOTTERS	D. Kaye	Motters	House and 148 acres farm	County road	$7,000	At station		7	2

COMMUTATION PASSENGER RATES.

Rates for Monthly and Monthly School-Tickets between Local Points,
excepting Baltimore Stations.

Miles.	Monthly, 54 Single Trips.	Monthly School, 46 Single Trips.	Miles.	Monthly, 54 Single Trips.	Monthly School, 46 Single Trips.	Miles.	Monthly, 54 Single Trips.	Monthly School, 46 Single Trips.
1	$2 00	$1 50	18	$7 05	$4 60	35	$9 55	$6 15
2	2 15	1 55	19	7 30	4 75	36	9 70	6 25
3	2 30	1 65	20	7 50	4 85	37	9 80	6 30
4	2 35	1 65	21	7 75	5 00	38	9 90	6 35
5	2 35	1 65	22	7 90	5 10	39	10 00	6 45
6	2 75	1 90	23	8 10	5 25	40	10 10	6 50
7	3 25	2 20	24	8 25	5 35	41	10 15	6 55
8	3 65	2 45	25	8 35	5 40	42	10 25	6 60
9	4 10	2 75	26	8 50	5 50	43	10 35	6 65
10	4 50	3 00	27	8 60	5 55	44	10 35	6 65
11	4 85	3 20	28	8 70	5 60	45	10 40	6 70
12	5 20	3 45	29	8 75	5 65	46	10 45	6 70
13	5 55	3 65	30	8 80	5 70	47	10 50	6 75
14	5 90	3 85	31	8 95	5 80	48	10 55	6 75
15	6 20	4 05	32	9 15	5 90	49	10 55	6 75
16	6 50	4 25	33	9 30	6 00	50	10 55	6 75
17	6 75	4 40	34	9 40	6 05			

Commutation Tickets, good for 30 Single Trips until used, and for an individual, his wife, minor children and servants, 2 cents per mile ; minimum $2.00.

Commutation School Tickets, good for 60 Single Trips until used, and limited to the children of the same parents, 1 cent per mile ; minimum $2.00. The children must be under 18 years of age, and actually attending school.

Monthly Tickets are limited to one individual and to 54 Single Trips, which must be taken in the *calendar* month for which ticket is issued.

Monthly School Tickets are limited to one individual and to 46 Single Trips, which must be taken in the *calendar* month for which ticket is issued. The individual must be under 18 years of age, and actually attending school.

1,000 Mile books, limited to one individual, or three of a family (residing together) or three of a firm or employees, or individual, wife, minor children or servants, $20.00.

Rates for Monthly and Monthly School-Tickets.

STATIONS.	From Hillen. Monthly	From Hillen. Monthly School.	From Fulton. Monthly	From Fulton. Monthly School.	STATIONS.	From Hillen. Monthly	From Hillen. Monthly School.	From Fulton. Monthly	From Fulton. Monthly School.
Highland Park	$4 15	$2 65	$2 15	$1 55	Avondale	$11 40	$7 15	$9 40	$6 05
Oakland	4 30	2 70	2 30	1 65	Medford	11 55	7 25	9 55	6 15
Arlington	4 35	2 70	2 35	1 65	Wakefield	11 70	7 30	9 70	6 25
Mt. Hope	4 35	2 70	2 35	1 65	New Windsor	11 80	7 40	9 80	6 30
Howardville	4 75	3 00	2 75	1 90	Linwood	12 15	7 60	10 15	6 55
Pikesville	5 65	3 55	3 65	2 45	Union Bridge	12 30	7 65	10 30	6 60
Mt. Wilson	6 10	3 80	4 10	2 75	Woodensburg	9 30	5 80	7 30	4 75
McDonogh	6 50	4 05	4 50	3 00	Fairview	9 75	6 10	7 75	5 00
G. S. Junction	6 85	4 30	4 85	3 20	Fowblesburg	9 90	6 20	7 90	5 10
Owings' Mills	7 20	4 50	5 20	3 45	Arcadia	10 25	6 40	8 25	5 35
Ginrich's	7 90	4 95	5 90	3 85	Hampstead	10 60	6 65	8 60	5 55
Timber Grove	8 20	5 15	6 20	4 05	Greenmount	10 70	6 70	8 70	5 60
St. George's	8 50	5 30	6 50	4 25	Maple Grove	10 80	6 75	8 80	5 70
Glyndon	8 75	5 50	6 75	4 40	Miller's	10 95	6 85	8 95	5 80
Emory Grove	8 75	5 50	6 75	4 40	Alesia	11 30	7 05	9 30	6 00
Glen Morris	8 75	5 50	6 75	4 40	Lineboro	11 70	7 30	9 70	6 25
Glen Falls	9 50	5 95	7 50	4 40	Intersection	11 80	7 40	9 80	6 30
Finksburg	9 50	5 95	7 50	4 85	Summit	11 90	7 45	9 90	6 35
Barrick's	9 90	6 20	7 90	5 10	Glenville	12 10	7 55	10 10	6 50
Patapsco	10 25	6 40	8 25	5 35	Green Ridge	12 15	7 60	10 15	6 55
Carrollton	10 50	6 55	8 50	5 50	South Branch	12 35	7 70	10 35	6 65
Tannery	10 70	6 70	8 70	5 60	Sinsheim	12 35	7 75	10 35	6 65
Westminster	10 95	6 85	8 95	5 80	Valley Junction	12 40	7 75	10 40	6 70
Spring Mills	11 30	6 95	9 30	5 90	Porter's	12 45	7 80	10 45	6 70

PROFILE
OF
W.M.R.R.
(MAIN LINE AND PORTION OF
B. & H. DIVISION.)

HORIZONTAL SCALE

VERTICAL SCALE

ENG. BY AM. BANK NOTE CO. N.Y.

42

ENGLAND & BRYAN,

Third and Vine Streets, Philadelphia,

Tanners, Curriers and Leather Manufacturers.

* * * * * * *

Tanners of the Celebrated "SCHLOSSER" Prime Oak Sole Leather,

WHICH RECEIVED THE HIGHEST PREMIUM AT THE

VIENNA, CENTENNIAL and NEW ORLEANS EXPOSITIONS.

* * * * * * *

Tannery located at TANNERY STATION, Carroll Co., Md., on the line of the Western Maryland Railroad.

BALTIMORE COAL CO.

DIGGS BROTHERS,

2 SOUTH STREET, AMERICAN BUILDING, BALTIMORE, MD.

DEALERS IN

COAL AND WOOD.

Cumberland, Despard, Cannel, Yok, Splint.

FANCY LUMP COAL FOR OPEN GRATES.

WILLIAM D. GILL,

LUMBER DEALER.

Georgia, North Carolina and Virginia Bill Stuff.

LARGE TIMBER

A SPECIALTY.

Flooring, Siding, Shingles, Laths, Palings, &c.

SASH, DOORS AND BLINDS,

AND BUILDING MATERIAL IN GENERAL.

Office : S. E. Corner President and Alice Anna Sts.

BALTIMORE, MD.

I carry a Larger Stock of Georgia and Virginia Yellow Pine of all kinds than any house in the trade.

ESTIMATES CHEERFULLY FURNISHED.   CORRESPONDENCE SOLICITED.

MORLING, MYER & CO.

Plain · and · Fancy

PRINTERS

Bookbinders, Stereotypers,

— AND —

BLANK BOOK MAKERS.

16 AND 18 NORTH STREET,

BALTIMORE.

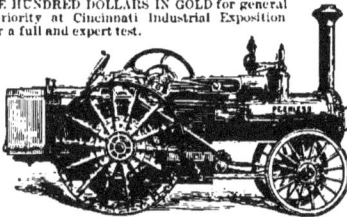

www.ingramcontent.com/pod-product-compliance
Lightning Source LLC
Chambersburg PA
CBHW031822090426
42739CB00008B/1376